Letts

English BASICS

FOR AGES 8-9
KEY STAGE 2

Contents

Verbs

Look and learn

The boy **kicked** the ball.

Many verbs are **doing** words.
They describe **actions**.

The boy **is** muddy.

Some verbs are **being** words.

Practice

Choose the best verb to complete each sentence.

are	yapped	invented	jumped	dug
left	dried	picked	learn	is

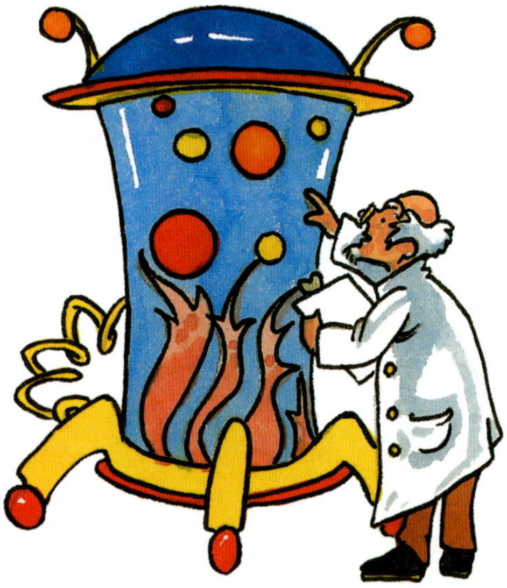

1. The professor ______________ a strange machine.
2. Shireen ______________ her hair with a towel.
3. We ______________ how to spell at school.
4. Tadpoles ______________ baby frogs.
5. In the summer it ______________ hot.
6. The toad ______________ out of the pond.
7. The man ______________ in a hurry.
8. I ______________ up the letters off the mat.
9. The lady ______________ her garden.
10. The little dog ______________ all day.

Challenge

The verbs in the sentences below are mixed up. Correct each verb.

1. A footballer ploughs. ___kicks___
2. A clown chops. ______________
3. A lumberjack bakes. ______________
4. A builder jokes. ______________
5. A shop assistant climbs. ______________
6. A cook saws. ______________
7. A teacher hammers. ______________
8. A mountaineer kicks. ______________
9. A carpenter prays. ______________
10. A priest sews. ______________
11. A tailor sells. ______________
12. A farmer teaches. ______________

Phonemes

Look and learn

A **phoneme** is the **smallest unit of sound** in a word.
A phoneme may be made up of **one or more letters** which make **one sound**.

The g**ir**l had c**ur**ly hair.

Practice

Choose the correct phoneme to complete each word.

1. ee ea s_ea_t	2. ai ay holid____	3. ow oa wind____	4. oo ow thr____
5. u oo p____sh	6. oy oi p____nt	7. ow ou h____l	8. aw au cl____
9. au or s____cer	10. ou ow l____d	11. ew oo f____d	12. oi oy enj____

Challenge

Think of three words containing the following phonemes:

1. **ir** (as in b**ir**d) ____________ ____________ ____________
2. **are** (as in sc**are**) ____________ ____________ ____________
3. **ea** (as in br**ea**d) ____________ ____________ ____________
4. **ur** (as in f**ur**) ____________ ____________ ____________
5. **ere** (as in th**ere**) ____________ ____________ ____________
6. **y** (as in fl**y**) ____________ ____________ ____________
7. **air** (as in f**air**) ____________ ____________ ____________

Verb tenses

Look and learn

Verbs can be written in different **tenses**.

Yesterday I **swam** in the sea.

This happened in the **past**. The verb is in the **past tense**.

Now I **am swimming** in the pool.

This is happening **now**. The verb is in the **present tense**.

Tomorrow I **will swim** in the river.

This will happen in the **future**. The verb is in the **future tense**.

Practice

Underline the verb in each sentence. Decide which tense it is in.

	past	present	future
1. I will go to bed early tonight.			✓
2. We drank all the lemonade.			
3. Alex is riding his bicycle.			
4. They crossed the busy street.			
5. Next week we will go on holiday.			
6. The car broke down.			
7. We gave the dog a bone.			
8. I will sleep in the tent in the summer.			
9. I am eating my dinner.			
10. Glen likes his sandwiches.			

Challenge

Write these sentences in the future tense.

1. I got up at six o'clock. I will get up at six o'clock.
2. I played with my friend. ____________
3. We rode our bikes to school. ____________
4. In the morning we did Maths. ____________
5. For lunch I had pizza. ____________
6. In the afternoon I painted a picture. ____________
7. I went to the shop after school. ____________
8. In the evening I watched TV. ____________

Syllables

Look and learn

When we say words slowly, we can hear how they may be broken down into **smaller parts** called **syllables**. Each syllable must contain at least **one vowel**.

gar – den

sun – shine

These words are both made of **two** syllables.

Practice

Add the syllables. Write the words you make.

1. den + tist = dentist

2. win + dow = ______

3. mag + net = ______

4. un + lock = ______

5. in + side = ______

6. sis + ter = ______

7. spi + der = ______

8. ti + ger = ______

9. ro + bot = ______

10. la + bel = ______

11. he + ro = ______

12. pu + pil = ______

Challenge

Join up the first and second syllable of each word.

1. pen	tern	
2. lan	nap	
3. trum	dent	
4. in	cils	pencils
5. kid	tor	
6. si	vent	
7. stu	cess	
8. tea	pet	
9. doc	cher	
10. prin	lent	

…fixes

Look and learn

A **suffix** is a **group of letters** we add to the **end of a word**.
A suffix changes the **meaning** of the word or the **job the word does**.

build → build**er**
(verb) (noun)

Practice

What do we call someone who:

1. paints? a painter
2. sings? ____
3. bakes? ____
4. gardens? ____
5. boxes? ____
6. skates? ____
7. reports? ____
8. cleans? ____
9. dances? ____
10. drums? ____
11. drives? ____
12. swims? ____

Challenge

Make these verbs into **er** or **or** nouns by adding the correct suffix.

1. trade trader
2. act ____
3. inspect ____
4 print ____
5. vote ____
6. visit ____
7. profess ____
8. edit ____
9. glide ____
10. sail ____

Alphabetical order

Look and learn

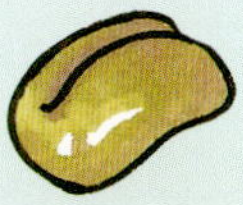

pa**p**er pa**v**ement pa**w** bea**n** bea**r** bea**t**

These words are arranged in alphabetical order according to their **third** letter.

These words are arranged in alphabetical order according to their **fourth** letter.

Practice

Arrange these words according to their third letter.

1. slip	slap	sleep		______________________
2. flick	flame	flock		______________________
3. prod	pray	prepare		______________________
4. shoulder	sharp	shut		______________________
5. drag	drum	drop	dry	______________________
6. beg	bee	beak	bell	______________________
7. cork	cost	coat	code	______________________
8. cheese	chip	chatter	chop	______________________
9. badge	base	baby	balloon	______________________
10. pet	pest	pear	pebble	______________________

Challenge

Think of a different letter to complete each word.
Then write the words in alphabetical order.

1. bea___t	bea___er	bea___en	______________________
2. can___le	can___l	can___on	______________________
3. com___uter	com___c	com___and	______________________
4. hel___ing	hel___o	hel___copter	______________________
5. scr___p	scr___b	scr___ll	______________________
6. str___ke	str___ngth	str___de	______________________

ophones

Look and learn

Homophones are words that **sound alike** but have **different spellings** and **different meanings**.

Ben **rode** along the **road** on his bike.

Practice

Join up the pairs of homophones.

ball	heard	bare	here	faint	their	find	fir
berth	hair	draft	check	flour	tide	steal	

hare	draught	birth	tied	fur	steel	cheque	
bear	fined	flower	there	herd	feint	bawl	hear

Challenge

Underline the words that are incorrectly spelled. Write the sentences correctly.

Last weak I thought I wood go for a sale on the see. I went down to the key, and maid my weigh to the boat. The tied was write inn.

Adverbs

Look and learn

Adverbs tell us **more about verbs**. Many adverbs tell us **how** something happened. Many adverbs end in **ly**.

The children are laughing **happily**.

Practice

Underline the verb and circle the adverb in each sentence.

1. The tortoise moved slowly.
2. Rain fell heavily.
3. Tom spoke rudely to his mother.
4. Shahla smiled sweetly.
5. The old man smacked his lips noisily.
6. Cross the road carefully.
7. I wrote my story neatly.
8. Angrily I kicked the ball away.
9. The lion growled fiercely.
10. In the sky the sun shone brightly.

Challenge

Match the adverbs with similar meanings.

1. wearily	timidly
2. bravely	clearly
3. shyly	sluggishly
4. happily	boisterously
5. distinctly	tiredly
6. sadly	cautiously
7. badly	unhappily
8. slowly	cheerfully
9. noisily	fearlessly
10. carefully	poorly

s within words

ook and learn

Look for **small words** within **longer words** to help you spell them.

Never be**lie**ve **lie**s.

Practice

friend	every	want	heard	brother
island	breakfast	hospital	separate	business

Which word contains:

1. land? ____________ **2.** bus? ____________

3. end? ____________ **4.** rat? ____________

5. broth? ____________ **6.** ear? ____________

7. spit? ____________ **8.** very? ____________

9. ant? ____________ **10.** break? ____________

Challenge

Find and write the ten long words in this puzzle. Underline a small word in each.

a	b	c	o	u	n	t	r	y	d	e	f
k	n	o	w	l	e	d	g	e	h	i	j
m	r	s	l	i	g	h	t	n	i	n	g
t	p	r	e	s	e	n	t	u	v	w	x
y	z	s	a	n	d	w	i	c	h	a	b
c	d	e	f	g	h	i	s	w	o	r	d
j	k	l	v	e	g	e	t	a	b	l	e
m	w	e	a	t	h	e	r	n	o	p	z
r	s	t	v	w	e	i	g	h	t	x	y
z	a	w	h	o	l	e	b	c	d	e	f

1. country

2. ____________

3. ____________

4. ____________

5. ____________

6. ____________

7. ____________

8. ____________

9. ____________

10. ____________

Adverbs again

Look and learn

clever – cleverly

We can just add **ly** to many root words.

happy – happily

If the word ends in **y**, we change the **y** to **i** and add **ly**.

gentle – gently

If the word ends in **e**, we drop the **e** and add **ly**.

Practice

Change these adjectives to adverbs.

	adjectives	adverbs
1.	glad	gladly
2.	slow	
3.	proud	
4.	hungry	
5.	lazy	
6.	merry	
7.	easy	
8.	simple	
9.	humble	
10.	horrible	

Challenge

Write the adjective from which each of these adverbs was made.

1. willingly willing **2.** gratefully ________ **3.** wearily ________

4. idly ________ **5.** miserably ________ **6.** skilfully ________

7. bravely ________ **8.** steadily ________ **9.** luckily ________

10. noisily ________ **11.** suddenly ________ **12.** truly ________

tives

ok and learn

An **adjective** is a **describing** word. It gives us more information about a **noun**.

The **brave** knight fought the **ugly** troll.

Practice

Choose the best adjective from the ladder to complete each sentence.

heavy
sad
nasty
choppy
sour
loud
howling
blunt
slippery
muddy

1. The lemon tasted very ___sour___.
2. When it rained the ground became ___________.
3. The case was too ___________ to lift.
4. The knife was very ___________.
5. There was a ___________ smell coming from the dustbin.
6. The ___________ eel got away.
7. The ___________ ending of the film made me cry.
8. The referee blew a ___________ blast on his whistle.
9. The ___________ sea made me feel sick.
10. The ___________ wind blew some trees down.

Challenge

Write a suitable adjective to go with each noun.

1. a ________ princess	**2.** a ________ giant	**3.** a ________ cave
4. a ________ cat	**5.** a ________ fire	**6.** a ________ owl
7. a ________ tree	**8.** a ________ monster	**9.** a ________ sheep
10. a ________ wood	**11.** a ________ cottage	**12.** a ________ necklace

Look and learn

A **simile** is when one thing is **compared** with another.

as busy as a bee

as slippery as a fish

Practice

Choose the best adjective from the wall to complete each simile.

soft	cool	flat	sweet
heavy	cold	red	slow
smooth	strong	light	gentle

1. as ___cold___ as ice
2. as __________ as honey
3. as __________ as silk
4. as __________ as a feather
5. as __________ as butter
6. as __________ as a pancake
7. as __________ as a dove
8. as __________ as a beetroot
9. as __________ as a cucumber
10. as __________ as iron
11. as __________ as a tortoise
12. as __________ as an ox

Challenge

Write a suitable noun to complete each simile.

1. as wise as an ___owl___
2. as fierce as a __________
3. as tall as a __________
4. as sharp as a __________
5. as hot as a __________
6. as old as a __________
7. as straight as a __________
8. as playful as a __________
9. as dry as a __________
10. as thin as a __________
11. as sour as __________
12. as rich as a __________

Common word endings

Look and learn

Look for **common letter patterns** to help you learn your spellings.

fl**are**

sc**are**

st**are**

Practice

Make and write these words.

f, m, n, r, s → ight

1. fight
2. ______
3. ______
4. ______
5. ______

fu, ba, do, bri, he → dge

6. ______
7. ______
8. ______
9. ______
10. ______

m, c, b, s, t → ore

11. ______
12. ______
13. ______
14. ______
15. ______

Challenge

Choose the correct ending from the box to complete each word.

1. should______ **2.** govern______

3. sta______ **4.** en______

5. cl______ **6.** bl______

7. sp______ **8.** ins______

9. ca______ **10.** appear______

word endings			
ure	tion	ough	
ear	ment	ire	ance
ould	ood	tch	

Comparing adjectives

Look and learn

Emma is **strong**.

Amy is **stronger**.

Shireen is the **strongest**.

When we **compare two nouns** we use a **comparative adjective**.

When we **compare three or more** nouns we use a **superlative adjective**.

Practice

Complete this chart.

	adjective	comparative adjective	superlative adjective
1.	light	lighter	
2.	fast		fastest
3.		rounder	
4.	soft		
5.			longest
6.		colder	
7.	smooth		
8.			slowest
9.		sharper	
10.	rough		

Challenge

Write the comparative and superlative form of each adjective. Take care with the spelling!

1. safe ___safer___ ___safest___

2. large ______ ______

3. tame ______ ______

4. hot ______ ______

5. thin ______ ______

6. sad ______ ______

7. heavy ______ ______

8. lucky ______ ______

9. ugly ______ ______

10. pretty ______ ______

Look and learn

A **suffix** is a **group of letters** we add to the **end of a word**. A suffix changes the **meaning** of the word or the **job** that the word does.

music – music**al**

Practice

Find ten nouns in the wordsearch. Make them into adjectives by adding the suffix **al**.

a	b	c	m	u	s	i	c	d	e
c	o	m	i	c	f	g	h	j	k
l	m	o	r	s	m	a	g	i	c
t	u	p	e	r	s	o	n	v	w
x	y	z	a	c	o	a	s	t	h
a	c	c	i	d	e	n	t	g	i
d	f	s	e	a	s	o	n	h	j
k	l	m	n	o	r	i	g	i	n
o	p	t	o	p	i	c	q	r	s
m	e	c	h	a	n	i	c	t	u

1. music ______ musical ______
2. ______ ______
3. ______ ______
4. ______ ______
5. ______ ______
6. ______ ______
7. ______ ______
8. ______ ______
9. ______ ______
10. ______ ______

Challenge

Choose the correct suffix to finish each word.

1. ment / tion — argu__ment__	**2.** ary / ic — athlet______	**3.** ic / ary — custom______
4. hood / ness — ill______	**5.** ship / hood — child______	**6.** ness / ship — leader______
7. ate / en — dark______	**8.** tion / ate — punctu______	**9.** ify / ise — horr______
10. en / ise — magnet______		

Gender words

Look and learn

Nouns may be classified according to their **gender**.

a girl

Nouns which refer to **females** are **feminine**.

a boy

Nouns which refer to **males** are **masculine**.

a teacher

Nouns which refer to **either** male or female are **common**.

Practice

Write each noun in the correct column in the chart.

queen boy uncle girl pupil husband friend teacher
king aunt wife doctor child niece nephew

masculine	feminine	common
	queen	

Challenge

Write each sentence. Change every masculine noun into a feminine noun.

1. My father was talking to my uncle. My mother was talking to my aunt.

2. The king looked at the prince. ______________________

3. The man told his son off. ______________________

4. My brother is going to be a policeman. ______________________

5. Lord Jones spoke to Mr Derby. ______________________

Contractions

Look and learn

We sometimes **shorten** a word by **leaving out** some letters. We use an **apostrophe** to show where letters have been left out.

I've = I have   don't = do not   I'll = I will

Practice

Match up each short word with its longer form.

1. we're	can not
2. wasn't	it is
3. can't	we are
4. don't	did not
5. didn't	was not
6. it's	do not

7. you're	we will
8. I'm	will not
9. we'll	you are
10. they've	she is
11. won't	they have
12. she's	I am

Challenge

Write each sentence. Write a short word to replace the underlined words.

1. It is a horribe day. It's a horrible day.
2. You have got a lovely hairstyle. ____________
5. The dog does not have a lead. ____________
4. He is cheating. ____________
5. We will do it later. ____________
6. I did not know what to do. ____________
7. They are his shorts. ____________
8. I would rather do it myself. ____________

Commas

Look and learn

The game, a cup final, was nearly over.

Commas are used to separate **extra bits** that are **added** to sentences.

Commas help to **break up** longer sentences **into smaller parts**.

Practice

Put the missing commas in each of these sentences.

1. Put on your coat Emma.
2. Sorry miss.
3. We'll go now shall we?
4. No don't do that!
5. The rabbit a white fluffy animal escaped from its cage.
6. I saw two children Sam and Peter in the shop.
7. To my surprise the children did not recognise me.
8. One of the trees the taller one had blown down.
9. The car a sports car was parked in the street near our house.

Challenge

Think of a sensible way to finish each of these sentences.

1. During the heavy rainstorm, ____________________
2. Because it was my birthday, ____________________
3. Even though I didn't feel like it, ____________________
4. Last of all, ____________________
5. A long time ago, before I was born, ____________________
6. A lady, the one with the dark hair, ____________________
7. My dog, my lovely, old dog, ____________________
8. The car, an old banger, ____________________

Word order

Look and learn

The man fried an egg.
The egg fried a man.

Sometimes when we **change the order of the words**, it **changes the meaning** of the sentence.

On Saturday I went shopping.
I went shopping on Saturday.

Sometimes we can change the order of the words and **not** change the meaning of the sentence.

Practice

Rearrange these words to make sensible sentences.

1. moo. Cows can ______ Cows can moo.
2. dog bones. My likes ______
3. fast. grey The runs horse ______
4. football. Yesterday played boy the ______
5. a The crashed into car wall. ______
6. workmen tea. drinking Some were ______
7. by town went We to bus. ______
8. noise. Bees a buzzing make ______
9. webs. their Spiders insects catch in ______
10. a long A tail. has mouse ______

Challenge

Change some words round. Make some silly sentences of your own.

1. The builder fell off the ladder. ______
2. A lady was watching the television. ______
3. The boy mowed the lawn. ______
4. Some children ate some crisps. ______
5. The singer played the guitar. ______
6. The clown wore some baggy trousers. ______
7. The teacher is reading a book. ______
8. The postman delivered a parcel. ______

Apostrophes marking possession

Look and learn

We use an **apostrophe** to show **ownership** (that something belongs to someone).

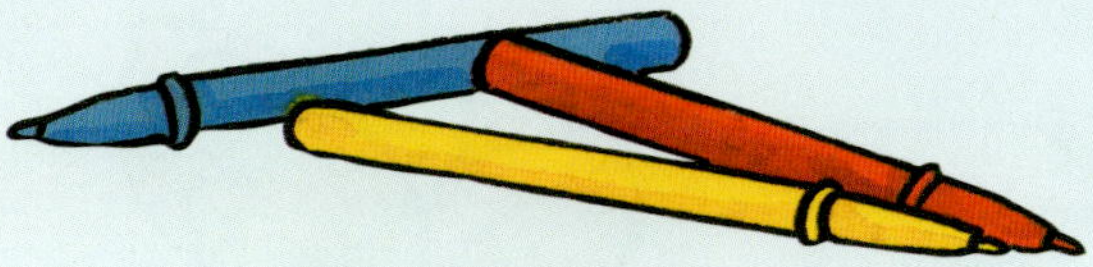

The girl's pens

The girls' pens

When there is only **one** owner, we usually write **'s**.

When there is **more** than one owner, we usually write **s'**.

Practice

Write the shortened form of each phrase.

1. the golfer's clubs — the clubs belong to the golfer
2. ______ — the hammer belongs to the builder
3. ______ — the boots belong to the footballer
4. ______ — the branches of the tree
5. ______ — the pen belongs to my uncle
6. ______ — the book belongs to my sister
7. ______ — the tractor belongs to the farmer
8. ______ — the glasses belong to Karen
9. ______ — the slippers belong to Mr Smith
10. ______ — the tail of the dinosaur

Challenge

Write what each of these phrase means.

1. the elephant's trunk — the trunk of the elephant
2. the elephants' ears ______
3. the sailors' ship ______
4. the ants' nest ______
5. the bird's eggs ______
6. the boys' books ______
7. the boys' bags ______
8. the teachers' room ______
9. the dogs' owner ______
10. the cat's eyes ______

Compound words

Look and learn

A **compound** word is made up of **two smaller words** joined together.

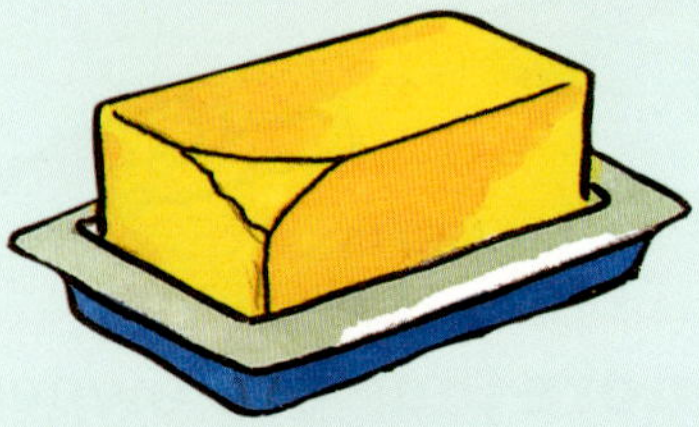

butter

+

fly

=

butterfly

Practice

Match up the words to make some compound words.

1. after	fast	
2. birth	sight	
3. break	way	
4. cloak	noon	afternoon
5. cup	step	
6. eye	room	
7. foot	card	
8. post	come	
9. motor	day	
10. over	board	

Challenge

Think of a word to go at the beginning or end of these words to make some more compound words.

1. ________work
2. rail________
3. table________
4. ________bow
5. round________
6. ________paper
7. ________fall
8. when________
9. some________
10. ________brush
11. hand________
12. ________hole

Diminutives

Look and learn

Diminutives are words that imply something **small**.

duck – duckling

sheep – lamb

A **diminutive** can sometimes be made by adding a **suffix**.

A **diminutive** can sometimes be a **different word altogether**.

Practice

Choose the correct diminutive for each animal.

calf	fawn	cub	chick	puppy
lamb	kitten	foal	kid	leveret

1. horse ___foal___ **2.** sheep ________

3. cat ________ **4.** dog ________

5. bear ________ **6.** goat ________

7. hen ________ **8.** deer ________

9. hare ________ **10.** cow ________

Challenge

Give each diminutive its correct suffix.

1. gos<u>ling</u>________ (ling/en)
2. eag________ (ling/let)
3. owl________ (let/en)
4. hill________ (kin/ock)
5. kitchen________ (ock/ette)
6. maid________ (ette/en)
7. duck________ (ling/let)
8. book________ (let/ling)
9. lamb________ (en/kin)
10. statu________ (ette/kin)

Say what each thing is.

A gosling is a small goose.

Surprising sounds

Look and learn

Letters don't always sound the way we expect them to!

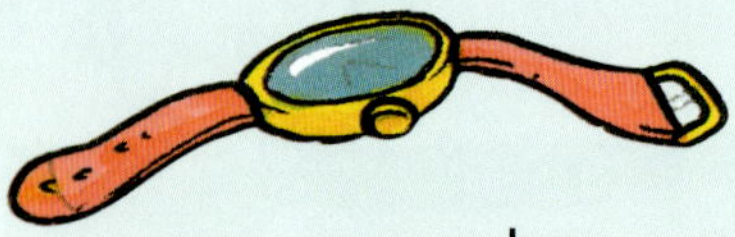

w**a**tch

Listen to the sound of **a** when it comes after **w**.

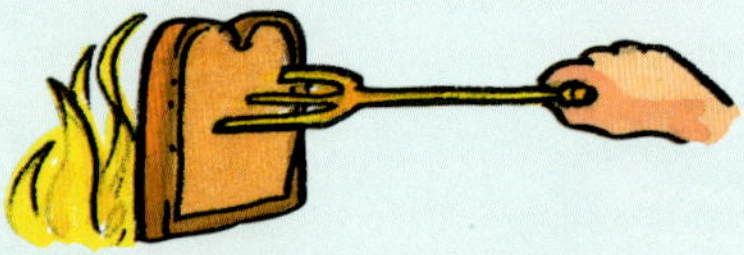

w**ar**m

Listen to the sound of **ar** when it comes after **w**.

w**or**k

Listen to the sound of **or** when it comes after **w**.

Practice

Choose the correct word to complete each sentence.

1. The early bird catches the ___worm___.
2. At school we have to __________ hard.
3. There are many different countries in our __________.
4. When the sun shines it is __________.
5. The vase was __________ a lot of money.
6. Most parents __________ their children about busy roads.
7. The __________ of bees left their hive.
8. My spelling seems to get __________ rather than better.
9. If you catch a thief you may get a __________.
10. The police had a __________ for the burglar's arrest.

war	wor
warm	world
warn	worth
warrant	worse
swarm	worm
reward	work

Challenge

Make these words. Circle the odd one out in each set.

1. c, b, d, w, cr + ash
___cash___
____
____
____
____

2. w, b, gr, st, l + and
____
____
____
____
____

3. g, gr, w, p, me + ander
____
____
____
____
____

4. b, w, m, h, l + atch
____
____
____
____
____

Types of sentences

Look and learn

There are **four** different **types of sentences**.

A **statement** gives **information**.

My car is red.

A **question asks** something.

Does it go fast?

A **command tells** someone to do something.

Get in.

An **exclamation** shows someone **feels something strongly**.

It's great!

Practice

Which type of sentence is each of these?

1. The door is open.
2. Have you seen my shorts?
3. What a lovely surprise!
4. Go and have a wash.
5. Where is Carla?
6. It was terrible!
7. I'm going out to play.
8. Keep quiet!
9. How old are you?
10. Come with me.

statement	question	command	exclamation
✓			

Challenge

Write these sentences and punctuate them correctly. After each sentence, write if it is a **statement** (S), **a question** (Q), **a command** (C) or **an exclamation** (E).

1. how far is it to the united states of america

_______________________________________ ( )

2. bring me my hat coat gloves and bag Philip

_______________________________________ ( )

3. im going to france for my holiday

_______________________________________ ( )

4. help theres a monster chasing me

_______________________________________ ( )

Experimenting with words

Look and learn

We can add **suffixes** to **some** types of words but not others.

look – looking – looked

We **can** add suffixes to **verbs**.

through

We **can't** add suffixes to **prepositions**.

Practice

Complete this chart.

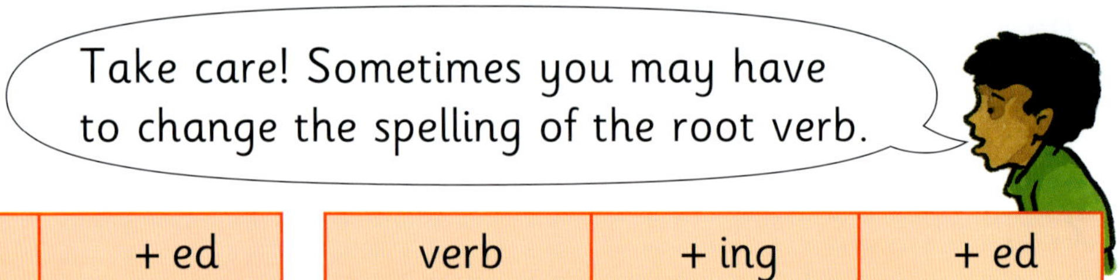

verb	+ ing	+ ed
1. wash	washing	washed
2. call		
3. bake		
4. clap		
5. climb		
6. dive		

verb	+ ing	+ ed
7. open		
8. joke		
9. nod		
10. breathe		
11. refuse		
12. tug		

Challenge

Write whether each word is a **verb** (V) or **preposition** (P).

1. break (V) **2.** behind ( )

3. into ( ) **4.** see ( )

5. over ( ) **6.** show ( )

7. think ( ) **8.** up ( )

9. towards ( ) **10.** from ( )

11. under ( ) **12.** teach ( )

Look and learn

The two common word endings **tion** and **sion** sometimes get confused.

conversation

television

The **tion** at the end of words sounds like **shun**.

The **sion** at the end of words sounds like **zhon**.

Practice

Write the noun that comes from each of these verbs.

tion	sion
examination	explosion
competition	decision
decoration	invasion
action	erosion
creation	confusion
preparation	division

1. invade invasion ______
2. decorate ______
3. prepare ______
4. confuse ______
5. explode ______
6. divide ______
7. examine ______
8. create ______
9. compete ______
10. decide ______
11. erode ______
12. act ______

Challenge

Mark this spelling test.

1. conclution	✗	2. information	☐
3. destrucsion	☐	4. revision	☐
5. inclusion	☐	6. generasion	☐
7. population	☐	8. sensasion	☐
9. composition	☐	10. incision	☐
11. propostition	☐	12. fracsion	☐

Write some words ending in **ssion.**

possession

______

______

______

The word endings able or ible

Look and learn

The two common word endings, **able** and **ible**, often get confused.

fashion + able = fashionable

It is often possible to see the root word when **able** is added.

horror + ible = horrible

It is **not** often possible to see the root word when **ible** is added.

Practice

Choose the best word to complete each sentence.

1. At home I am responsible for doing the washing up.
2. The archaeologist made a ______________ discovery.
3. I like to wear ______________ clothes.
4. My favourite armchair is very ______________.
5. I made a ______________ mistake.
6. It is ______________ to win the lottery – but not likely!
7. When something disappears it is ______________.
8. When I am sad I feel quite ______________.
9. It is not ______________ to run across the road.
10. The opposite of unreasonable is ______________.

able	ible
comfortable	possible
reasonable	terrible
fashionable	responsible
remarkable	sensible
miserable	invisible

Challenge

Choose **able** or **ible** to complete each word.

1. flex ible
2. understand______________
3. laugh______________
4. incred______________
5. aud______________
6. agree______________
7. punish______________
8. obtain______________
9. favour______________
10. indel______________
11. divis______________
12. change______________

Look and learn

Some **letter strings** are very **common** – but they do not always make the same sound!

cough

tough

bough

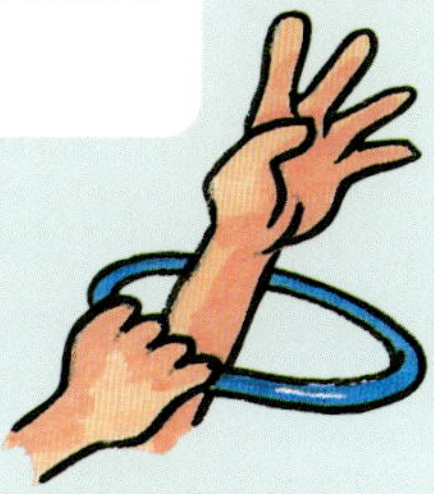

through

Practice

Write the pairs of words that contain the same letter strings.

trough	grow
post	shoulder
allow	look
hour	gone
could	give
one	though
bear	have
five	hear
soon	cost
wave	pour

1. ______________
2. ______________
3. ______________
4. ______________
5. ______________
6. trough though
7. ______________
8. ______________
9. ______________
10. ______________

Challenge

Make up some sentences. Use each pair of words in a sentence.

1. moth mother **Mother** caught the **moth** in the net.
2. office mice ______________
3. glove move ______________
4. die believe ______________
5. snow cow ______________
6. case vase ______________
7. line machine ______________
8. wallet mallet ______________

Conjunctions

Look and learn

A **conjunction** is a joining word. It may be used to join **two sentences**.

It was raining. I put up my umbrella.
(two sentences)

It was raining **so** I put up my umbrella.
(one sentence with a conjunction)

Practice

Make these pairs of sentences into one sentence.
Choose the best conjunction from the words in brackets.

1. The lion looked fierce. It was tame. (but/and/so)
   The lion looked fierce but it was tame.
2. I hurt my ankle. I fell off my bike. (and/so/when)
   ____
3. I went to bed early. I was tired. (whether/so/because)
   ____
4. It rained hard. I got soaked. (and/because/if)
   ____
5. Sharif did his spellings. He got them all right. (but/and/when)
   ____
6. The birds flew away. A cat was after them. (and/because/so)
   ____

Challenge

Think of a suitable ending for each sentence. Underline the conjunctions in each.

1. Sam's favourite food is pizza <u>but</u> ____________________
2. I went home when ____________________
3. I had to stay in so ____________________
4. It became very cold because ____________________
5. Alice put on her swimming costume and ____________________
6. Mr Patel turned off the television when ____________________
7. This is the naughty boy who ____________________
8. We ran across the bridge which ____________________

Positive and negative

Look and learn

This is a **positive** sentence. It means **yes**.

This is a **negative** sentence. It means **no**. The main negative is **not** or **n't**.

Practice

Say whether each sentence is positive (✓) or negative (✗).

1. I love snakes. ✓
2. I don't like spelling. ______
3. We are not allowed to stay up late. ______
4. Chantel is good at climbing. ______
5. This is the best ice cream ever. ______
6. New York is not in Canada. ______
7. Poor Sarah is not very well. ______
8. I can't say the alphabet backwards. ______
9. I hate sprouts. ______
10. My favourite hobby is collecting stamps. ______

Challenge

Write each of these negative sentences and make each one positive.

1. Elizabeth is not a girl. Elizabeth is a girl.
2. Don't wear your old clothes. ______
3. You are not allowed to swim here. ______
4. It is not very fair. ______
5. Justin can't play the piano. ______
6. It is not raining today. ______
7. Shirley was not able to do the sum. ______
8. You shouldn't wave at me. ______
9. The sea wasn't very warm. ______
10. Hedgehogs don't have prickly spines. ______

Answers

Page 2
Practice: 1. invented, 2. dried, 3. learn, 4. are, 5. is, 6. jumped, 7. left, 8. picked, 9. dug, 10. yapped
Challenge: answers may vary

Page 3
Practice: 2. holiday, 3. window, 4. throw, 5. push, 6. point, 7. howl, 8. claw, 9. saucer, 10. loud, 11. food, 12. enjoy
Challenge: answers may vary

Page 4
Practice:
past: 2. drank, 4. crossed, 6.broke down, 7. gave
present: 3. is riding, 9. am eating, 10. likes
future: 5. will go, 8. will sleep
Challenge:
2. I will play with my friend.
3. We will ride our bikes to school.
4. In the morning we will do Maths.
5. For lunch I will have pizza.
6. In the afternoon I will paint a picture.
7. I will go to the shop after school.
8. In the evening I will watch TV.

Page 5
Practice: 2. window, 3. magnet, 4. unlock, 5. inside, 6. sister, 7. spider, 8. tiger, 9. robot, 10. label, 11. hero, 12. pupil
Challenge: 2. lantern, 3. trumpet, 4. invent, 5. kidnap, 6. silent, 7. student, 8. teacher, 9. doctor, 10. princess

Page 6
Practice: 2. singer, 3. baker, 4. gardener, 5. boxer, 6. skater, 7. reporter, 8. cleaner, 9. dancer, 10. drummer, 11. driver, 12. swimmer
Challenge: 2. actor, 3. inspector, 4. printer, 5. voter, 6. visitor, 7. professor, 8. editor, 9. glider, 10. sailor

Page 7
Practice:
1. slap/sleep/slip
2. flame/flick/flock
3. pray/prepare/prod
4. sharp/shoulder/shut
5. drag/drop/drum/dry
6. beak/bee/beg/bell
7. coat/code/cork/cost
8. chatter/cheese/chip/chop
9. baby/badge/balloon/base
10. pear/pebble/pest/pet

Challenge:
1. beast/beaten/beaver
2. canal/candle/cannon
3. comic/command/computer
4. helicopter/hello/helping
5. scrap/scroll/scrub
6. strength/stride/stroke

(some answers may vary)

Page 8
Practice: tide/tied, ball/bawl, heard/herd, bare/bear, here/hear, faint/feint, their/there, find/fined, berth/birth, hair/hare, draft/draught, flour/flower, check/cheque, steal/steel, fir/fur
Challenge: Last week I thought I would go for a sail on the sea. I went down to the quay and made my way to the boat. The tide was right in.

Page 9
Practice: 2. fell (verb) heavily (adverb), 3. spoke (verb) rudely (adverb), 4. smiled (verb) sweetly (adverb), 5. smacked (verb) noisily (adverb), 6. cross (verb) carefully (adverb), 7. wrote (verb) neatly (adverb), 8. angrily (adverb) kicked (verb), 9. growled (verb) fiercely (adverb), 10. shone (verb) brightly (adverb)
Challenge: 2. bravely/fearlessly, 3. shyly/timidly, 4. happily/cheerfully, 5. distinctly/clearly, 6. sadly/unhappily, 7. badly/poorly, 8. slowly/sluggishly, 9. noisily/boisterously, 10. carefully/cautiously

Page 10
Practice: 1. island, 2. business, 3. friend, 4. separate, 5. brother, 6. heard, 7. hospital, 8. every, 9. want, 10. breakfast
Challenge: 2. knowledge, 3. lightning, 4. present, 5. sandwich, 6. sword, 7. vegetable, 8. weather, 9. weight, 10. whole (some answers may vary)

Page 11
Practice: 2. slowly, 3. proudly, 4. hungrily, 5. lazily, 6. merrily, 7. easily, 8. simply, 9. humbly, 10. horribly
Challenge: 2. grateful, 3. weary, 4. idle, 5. miserable, 6. skilful, 7. brave, 8. steady, 9. lucky, 10. noisy, 11. sudden, 12. true

Page 12
Practice: 2. muddy, 3. heavy, 4. blunt, 5. nasty, 6. slippery, 7. sad, 8. loud, 9. choppy, 10. howling
Challenge: answers may vary

Page 13
Practice: 2. sweet, 3. smooth, 4. light, 5. soft, 6. flat, 7. gentle, 8. red, 9. cool, 10. heavy, 11. slow, 12. strong
Challenge: answers may vary

Page 14
Practice: 2. might, 3. night, 4. right, 5. sight, 6. fudge, 7. badge, 8. dodge, 9. bridge, 10. hedge, 11. more, 12. core, 13. bore, 14. sore, 15. tore
Challenge: 2. government, 3. station, 4. enough, 5. clear, 6. blood, 7. spire, 8. insure, 9. catch, 10. appearance

Page 15
Practice: 1. lightest, 2. faster, 3. round/roundest, 4. softer/softest, 5. long/longer, 6. cold/coldest, 7. smoother/smoothest, 8. slow/slower, 9. sharp/sharpest, 10. rougher/roughest
Challenge: 2. larger/largest, 3. tamer/tamest, 4. hotter/hottest, 5. thinner/thinnest, 6. sadder/saddest, 7. heavier/heaviest, 8. luckier/luckiest, 9. uglier/ugliest 10. prettier/prettiest

Page 16
Practice: 2. comic/comical, 3. magic/magical, 4. person/personal, 5. coast/coastal, 6. accident/accidental, 7. season/seasonal, 8. origin/original, 9. topic/topical, 10. mechanic/mechanical
Challenge: 2. athletic, 3. customary, 4. illness, 5. childhood, 6. leadership, 7. darken, 8. punctuate, 9. horrify, 10. magnetise

Page 17
Practice:
masculine: boy/uncle/husband/king/nephew
feminine: queen/girl/aunt/wife/niece
common: pupil/friend/teacher/doctor/child
Challenge:
2. The queen looked at the princess.
3. The woman told her daughter off.
4. My sister is going to be a policewoman.
5. Lady Jones spoke to Mrs Derby.

Page 18
Practice: 2. was not, 3. can not, 4. do not, 5. did not, 6. it is, 7. you are, 8. I am, 9. we will, 10. they have, 11. will not, 12. she is
Challenge:
2. You've got a lovely hairstyle.
3. The dog doesn't have a lead.
4. He's cheating.
5. We'll do it later.
6. I didn't know what to do.
7. They're his shorts.
8. I'd rather do it myself.

Page 19
Practice:
1. Put on your coat, Emma.
2. Sorry, miss.
3. We'll go now, shall we?
4. No, don't do that!
5. The rabbit, a white fluffy animal, escaped from its cage.
6. I saw two children, Sam and Peter, in the shop.
7. To my surprise, the children did not recognise me.
8. One of the trees, the taller one, had blown down.
9. The car, a sports car, was parked in the street, near our house.

Challenge: answers may vary